ANCHOR BOOKS

LAZY DAYS AND SUNSHINE RAYS

Edited by

Natalie Nightingale

First published in Great Britain in 2001 by
ANCHOR BOOKS
Remus House,
Coltsfoot Drive,
Peterborough, PE2 9JX
Telephone (01733) 898102

HB ISBN 1 85930 943 7
SB ISBN 1 85930 948 8

FOREWORD

Lazy Days And Sunshine Rays is an enchanting collection children are sure to enjoy. The poems range from funny, light-hearted verses to thoughtful poetry generated by the world around us.

The poets range in their styles, approach and age. Each poem has something equally delightful to offer, however, I'm sure you'll have your own personal favourite.

Lazy Days And Sunshine Rays is guaranteed to be a well read book and inspiration for the child in your life.

Natalie Nightingale
Editor

CONTENTS

WOULD YOU LIKE TO COME TO TEA?

Would you like to come to tea?
We'll eat at half-past four.
I'm not sure what we'll have yet,
but I'll be 'Mum' and pour!

Perhaps I'll make a salad,
from dandelion leaves.
With marigold petals for colour
and nectar sauce if you please!

Or maybe we could have worm cake?
They wriggle so delightfully you know!
You don't fancy that today dear?
Well perhaps I'll leave them in the mud to grow!

I've got a little saucepan,
with some of Mummy's cold tea.
I thought if I stirred in some clover heads,
it would taste better for you and me!

I managed to find some toadstools,
and turned them upside down.
They looked like little pizzas
decorated with buttercup petals and thistledown!

What about rose petal ice cream?
Or maybe fairy delight?
I keep on forgetting how to make them . . .
I hope I can get them right!

Perhaps my darling Mother,
will take pity on me.
She'll make a splendid picnic tea
for my dollies, my teddy and me!

Margi Hughes

NEVER AGAIN

I went to a birthday party,
It was for my friend,
When I got there, I felt shy,
But I stayed until the end.
I can't say I was sorry
In fact I felt quite glad,
Because if you listen carefully
I'll tell you what I had . . .
I had trifle and sandwiches
And fruitcake and buns,
And ice cream and chocolate
And lots of pop and sponge.
A lollipop and sweets
And some jelly babies, too.
Suddenly I felt queasy
And my tummy wasn't right
Mum had to come and fetch me
And I was ill all night.
I could see that Mum felt cross,
But she didn't say too much,
She knew I'd never face again
All that chocolate and such.
I knew she could see
That I did feel very rotten,
And I'd never ever do it again,
So everything's forgotten.

Bronwen Gould

THE TORTOISE AND THE CAT

I bought a little tortoise
His name was Tinky Pooh
Topsie did not like him, he didn't know what to do
When Tinky Pooh began to crawl
Topsie ran up the garden wall
There he stayed for several hours
Till Tinky Pooh hid among the flowers
Topsie came down, it was time to be fed
I put Tinky Pooh out of sight in the shed
In the garden next day they came face to face
Made friends with each other and planned a race
Topsie went off full-steam ahead
Tinky Pooh only got a foot from the shed
Topsie meowed 'I won! I won!'
Tinky Pooh murmured 'Well done! Well done!'
Now the best of friends are we
Tinky Pooh, Topsie and me.

Therese Spare

SAMUEL AND SUSAN

*(A true story told to me by Sue, now a grown-up
and Grandma to Charlotte)*

There once was a boy called Samuel White,
Who *never* did wrong, he *always* did right.
Always the first to finish his work,
He smiled at the class with a satisfied smirk.
When someone was naughty it wasn't too long
Till Sam told the teacher just who'd done what wrong.
Now in the same class was a girl I'll call Sue.
(I've changed both their names, but the story is true.)
And Sue couldn't stomach this Samuel White:
She was longing to punch him and have a good fight.
The others disliked goody Samuel too,
So then they all issued a challenge to Sue.
'We'll give you a packet of mints,' they all said,
'If you'll get the rice pudding all over his head.'
At last the day came that they'd longed for so much -
Rice pudding with jam was served up for lunch.
And then as she stirred the jam round in the pud
Sue heard a loud voice - she'd been sure that she would.
'You ought not to do that!' friend Samuel said.
For once he'd done wrong, for our Susan saw red.
He kept on at Sue, and he wouldn't desist.
Sue thought of the mints, and she couldn't resist.
She shoved his head down - and smug little Sam
Was plastered with sticky rice pudding and jam.

Jennifer Bailey

MEONA REECE

Meona Reece, what a funny and unusual name,
unlike a common Sarah, Clare or plain old Jane.
The meo- is like meow and she is often called Cat,
the Reece is like geese and she's never liked that.
This young girl of height 4 feet 2,
has large beautiful eyes that are deep sea blue.
Short ginger, spiky hair,
that is styled in such a way to cause people to stare.
For this girl Meona is known to be very mysterious,
always funny and sometimes serious.
She is bubbly, full of excitement and fun,
and goes on every fantastic adventure under the sun.
Popular at school with her teachers and friends,
excellent at her studies and her help she often lends.
To those in need and those all alone,
and will often bring them to slumber parties at her home.
Her life is full of laughter every day,
and she is well-known for the flute she does play.
Such beautiful melodies are often heard,
The songs that she plays are like the sound of a bird.
A wonderful girl, can she have a round of applause please,
I give you the amazing, the extraordinary, Meona Reece!

Samantha Drewry

WHAT IS HEAVEN LIKE?

What is Heaven like
Is it all pink and frothy white?
Does the man at the gate
Let you in if you're late?
Or send you back for another flight!

And what of the other place
Where you go when in deep disgrace?
Has he horns and a tail?
Does he have to be male?
Does he send you out flying in space?

Is it like going up in a balloon?
Is it farther than the moon?
Though I wonder a lot
I prefer what I've got
Cos I *don't* want to go there too soon.

J Lodge

STRANGER WITH BANJO

He came across the meadow
with a banjo in his hand.
Rumpti-iddity, rumpti-iddity -
nothing was ever so grand;
such liquidity: rumpti-iddity,
rumpti-iddity. Twang!

He told me his name was Tom Tully.
His music came out of the ground,
Rumpti-iddity, rumpti-iddity -
there was magic in the sound.
He'd sing me a ditty - rumpti-iddity,
rumpti-iddity - for a pound!

I gave him a pound and he sang
in a tongue that I'd never heard:
Rumpti-iddity, rumpti-iddity;
I understood not a word.
Flibbertygibbety, rumpti-iddity,
rumpti-iddity - slurred!

I asked him 'What means this strange song?'
and was he a witch, or magician.
Rumpti-iddity, rumpti-iddity.
He assumed an unusual position
of lifeless rigidity. Rumpti-iddity,
rumpti-iddity. Derision!

I gave him a pound for his pains.
He sang me his ditty and then:
Rumpti-iddity, rumpti-iddy:
'I'm not from the world of men.'
No trace of timidity. Rumpti-iddity,
rumpti-iddity. Never again!

Adrian Brett

EXCUSES, EXCUSES

I have thought up a brilliant racket -
one that promises to make a packet!

I'm forging notes for the children at school
and my inspiration would make you drool . . .
Like
'Claude cannot be at school today
I'm afraid the psychiatrist locked him away'
Or
'Wayne is unfortunately very ill -
the doctors will have to prescribe him a pill
But research may take them eight months, or nine
so he won't be back for a very long time'
Then
'Henrietta is stricken with mumps:
her neck's come out in awfully big lumps!
No visitors should try to call
She is infectious, after all'
But my favourite excuse has got to be
the one for mistaken identity . . .
'Your Truant Officer called to enquire
about a boy called Horace Maguire
We have *no* children - he doesn't live here
Perhaps the teachers have been on the beer?'

Five quid a letter is my modest fee -
we should be millionaires by 2003!

Bazil Bratt, aged 9

Author's note: If you knew Claude, you'd realise
                    I didn't have to stretch the truth too much!

Bazil Bratt (9)

A CAUTIONARY TALE

(Written for my grandson, aged 4 years, who while on holiday in France opposite 'Belle Ile' seemed to live on fresh air, although fit and active)

Once there was a little boy, I think his name was Peter,
He didn't like his food, and was a very poor eater.
His sister Bella loved her food and ate up all her dinner,
But Peter just went out to play and steadily grew thinner.
One day, a fierce wind came along and thought 'I'll play a trick',
It took a peep at Peter who, by now, looked like a stick.
It lifted him, and tossed him right up into the air.
He landed on an island, but the wind, it didn't care.
His daddy was left on the beach just holding Peter's coat,
He said, 'I'll run down to the port and hire a little boat.'
He rowed and rowed and rowed until he reached the distant shore
To look for Peter who, by now, was very thin and poor.
His daddy really was upset, and in a state of shock,
But then, he thought he saw a stick hiding behind a rock.
Well, it was Peter, cowed and scared, his body all a-quivering.
Dad picked him up and cuddled him to stop the poor lad shivering.
He rowed him back to Mummy, who was waiting on the shore.
She said, 'There's nothing in your tummy, you really must eat more.'
Well, after that, they couldn't find enough for him to eat.
He ate some eggs, he ate some fish, he even ate some meat.
He ate some greens, he ate some fruit, he grew so big and tall,
He was bigger than his daddy who could not believe it all.
And when the fierce wind came along to play another trick,
It couldn't lift up Peter, who just laughed till he was sick!

J P Taylor

HOW WE FIND FRIENDS

Whoopee . . . Summer's break is here,
The joy of getting up early with the lark,
Today some are going out for the day,
Yes, some to the seaside or the park.

Ideal each day is for you,
And some friends to find too,
By sharing the goes on the swing,
So too, your goes down the slide,
Sharing lots does teach.

Last year I watched two little girls,
Talking and taking turns without fuss,
And by this a friendship grew,
Today they are truly friends,
They see each other three times a week,
That chance turned them into lasting mates.

Like a friend I once found,
Our friendship walks on firm ground,
There is only a days difference of age,
Her daughter my Godchild,
My younger one hers . . . like sisters to be,
When in need each other consult,
A lifetime friendship we both say the result.

That is how I pray for all of you,
Happiness and friendships, to come true,
Once doing my voluntary aid, asking for no reward,
But lots of happiness and joy,
Is what can be scored, *'God bless you all'*,
Around the globe may your generation see a future light,
And it bring 'A nice world full of delight'.

Anita M Slattery

BEING ME

I like to be silly and very rude,
Stomp around with real attitude.
My mother says I should behave
Like sister, 'Goody Two Shoes Mave'.
Boring is something that I am not
So cancel that with one large swot!
What is the point of being quiet
When you can shout and cause a riot?
People know when I'm around
Many often seem to tut and frown,
But then they are usually extremely old
And expect everyone to do as they are told.
Well bully for them and all that stuff
If they don't like me then that is tough.
Watch this space if you want to see action
I know the buttons to push to get a reaction.
As dear sister always acts so sweet and kind
I wonder what does go on in that girl's mind,
Something else must live in there
Beside Barbie dolls and yellow hair.
Enough of her let's talk about me
For I am top of this family tree.
What people say about me is not true,
Believe me or I'll shout until I am blue.
Before I end my personal history
There is one strange and odd mystery,
Why do my family think I am moody and mean
Isn't everyone when they become thirteen?

Vivienne Doncaster

TALE AS OLD AS TIME

There was once a girl called Belle
Her friends thought she was swell
As well as being pretty
She was also quite witty
And her breath was stinky as well

Belle went in search of a castle
Her horse was adorned with a tassel
The prospect of riches
Left her in stitches
A knight shouldn't be too much hassle

But when she met her Prince Charming
His appearance was rather alarming
Gruesome, hairy
And incredibly scary
His skin seemed to need farming

The Beast felt some hope in his heart
But only Belle could make a start
Love is a trial
It lasts for a while
But first Cupid must shoot the dart

And life is not always fair
Belle was a tough old mare
The Beast's kindly ways
Ceased to amaze
So she made a carpet from his hair

And that is the age-old story
Told in its unedited glory
Beauty and the Beast -
A smart girl gets to feast
Well, you said you wanted it gory!

Meghan Graham

WOMEN'S WAYS

Scratch, scratch beneath the floorboards,
Pitter-patter through the house,
Scratch, scratch, moving upwards,
Quick! hide the cheese we've got a mouse.

Up the stairs, the youngest daughter,
On a chair inside her flat,
Begging, screaming, near hysterics,
Fiancé runs to get the cat.

Brings in pussy, sets her hunting,
Tail and whiskers all atwitch,
Along the skirting, creeping, jumping,
Prey is caught without a hitch.

'Stop him Darling, he will kill it!
Look! how it trembles, oh! - poor thing,
Oh! - you horrid, wicked pussy,
As for you, sir keep your ring.'

In the pub his brain awhirling,
Orders quick a large Guinness,
Still can't grasp the female logics,
That has left him loverless.

So! Take heed sir if you're courting,
Don't take deposit on a house,
Until you're absolutely certain,
She's not frightened of a mouse.

Joe Holloway

WITCH WAY

With a swish, swish, swish,
High into the sky
Rides the daredevil witch
As she learns to fly.

She's a fearsome sight
On her broomstick steed,
And the other witches
Are quite agreed
That she's not really safe
Up there at all,
But, laughing, she dives,
And just misses a wall!

She goes far too fast,
Skims the tops of trees,
And her L-plates drop off
'Midst a swarm of bees,
Then she zigzags over
Some terrified sheep,
Who bump into each other
And fall in a heap!

'This is fun,' she cries,
In a spiralling drop,
'But my problem is -
I can't make it stop!'

Ivy Lee

THE FROGLING FRAMBOREE

They were prancing, they were dancing,
Quite ecstatic in the rain,
Jumping without bumping,
Up and down then up again.
Little ones and larger ones
All joining in the fun,
The local friendly Framboree
For froglings had begun.
As droplets dripped and splished about
In plopping puddles everywhere,
The frogling king in robe of green,
His golden crown so proudly worn,
Accompanied his lady queen
Towards the lakeside lawn.

The rain fell faster, drumming beat,
Croakings crescendoed joyfully,
The sky split wide with lightning flash
As frogling bands played merrily.
Thunder cracked and crashed at will
Above the lake about the trees,
Bodies throbbed in froggy thrill,
Leaping legs leapt higher still.
Suddenly, a final clap,
Torrents tumbled down no more,
Showers stilled, all was calm,
Movement ceased upon the shore.
Faint glimmer showed the light of dawn,
A signal from his majesty,
Froglings massed for one last leap
Into the lake's deep secrecy.

C Mansfield

DAISY MAY

There was a little pony,
Her name was Daisy May,
Her mane and tail were white as snow,
Her coat was dapple grey.

Taking turns to ride her
As she trotted down the street,
All the children loved her
She was so kind and sweet.

They brushed her and they groomed her,
They made her dapples glow,
They took her to a country fair
Where she won Best In Show.

Christine A Lee

NAUGHTY NELL

This is the story of Naughty Nell
Who always pretended she was unwell.
Upon her friends she cast a spell,
They were too frightened of her to tell.
She wished upon them frightful things
Like falling off the slides and swings.
She didn't think that she was bad
Which was so very, very sad.
Was there hope she'd mend her ways
Unfortunately not, because her days
Were spent thinking of annoying ways,
To spoil the other children's days.
She frightened them with spiders and bugs
And dropped dead mice into their milk mugs.
There was no end to her evil deeds,
They sprang from her like growing weeds.
It is no wonder Naughty Nell - so bad -
Was left without a friend - alone and sad.

Betty Harper

Dog's Laugh

Brock just hates to be alone;
He reckons it's written in runes of stone -
'Great is the need
For dogs to lead'.
So when we're scattered
(As if it mattered!)
He goes indoors and roars!
And with broadest grin
He watches as I come galloping in -
'Nice to see you come to heel,
You know the warning wasn't real.'
I can usually tell if there's someone there
By the crescendo of the shouts 'Beware!'
But sometimes I know it's just for fun -
He likes to see me come at a run!

Eileen M Lodge

MATTHEW CHRISTOPHER

Matthew Christopher said to me,
'I'd like sausages for tea,'
'The cupboard's bare' I said to him,
'We'll have to visit farmer Jim.

The farm is only down the lane,
Let's just hope it doesn't rain,
We'll put our coat and wellies on,
And take a trip, we won't be long.'

'Bow, wow, wow!' the farm dog said
As we approached, his name is Jed.
A pussycat was standing by,
'Miaow' she said and jumped up high.

'Cluck, cluck, cluck' it sounds like hens,
Laying eggs outside in pens.
'Cock-a-doodle, don't be late,'
The rooster flies up on the gate.

'Baa, baa, baa' sheep on the lawn,
Their woolly coats to keep them warm.
In the fields the moo-cows sit,
Their milk we drink to keep us fit.

Grunting, snorting pigs in sties,
'Oink, oink, oink' as we walk by.
'Neigh' the farm horse stands up proud
And views the farm from all around.

Matthew Christopher said to me,
'I don't want sausages for tea,
I think I'll just have jam and bread,
then I 'xpect it's time for bed.'

Jane Birch

MATTHEW'S ENCHANTED WALLPAPER

As Matthew climbed into bed,
His mother kissed him goodnight.
She brushed back the hair from his forehead,
Smiled sweetly and said 'Sleep tight.'

He gave a big yawn and turned over,
As the darkness began to creep.
Matthew didn't need any rocking
And was very soon fast asleep.

Now on Matthew's bedroom wallpaper,
There were pictures of old-fashioned scenes.
With castles and mountains, forests and lakes,
Brave knights and dragons, royal princes and queens.

But just as the chimes struck midnight
On the grandfather clock in the hall,
All the characters came to life
On Matthew's bedroom wall.

A knight sat astride a dragon,
Rode up and reached out his hand,
Lifted Matthew onto its back
And flew off into a strange land.

They flew over mountains and forests,
'Tween the dragon's wings Matthew squat.
Then fairy tale spires came into view,
'Twas the castle of Camelot.

Matthew's mum gently shook him.
'Come on now, you sleepy head.
I thought I would never wake you,
It's time to get out of bed.'

'Good morning,' said Matthew.
'Guess where I've been!
To meet King Arthur
And Guinevere, his queen.'

Ian Fyles

POLLY THE BRENT GOOSE

Polly the Brent goose with the injured wing lay on the top of the beach,
Polly felt ill and couldn't move and her friends were out of reach.

John saw Polly as he walked with Jess, his dog along the shore,
They didn't walk too far as Jess's feet would get sore.

John noticed the goose hadn't moved far when they returned
from their walk,
John told Jess to sit and stay while he saw to the goose and
quietly talked.

John comforted the goose and picked her up and wrapped her in
his coat,
John took Jess by the lead and they walked home and passed the old
shipwrecked boat.

At home at the old cottage John saw to the injured goose.
John asked his friend Ted the vet to examine the goose
to see if he could help.

Ted treated Polly and said she would soon be well once more.
Then John could take Polly back to her friends on the sea shore.
Ted told John how to feed and care for Polly.

John's mother used to talk to Polly and so did John's friend Molly,
they talked very quietly to the goose and they thought she looked
quite jolly.

Soon Polly was much stronger and John could keep her no longer.
It was nearly time for Polly and her friends to leave England
and return to the islands off the north coast of Russia.
Every year they left in June and would fly away under a beautiful
full moon.

John took Polly back to the shore, he gently put her down near where
she was found.
A group of geese soon gathered round and welcomed Polly with a
special sound.

Next day when John and Jess came down to the beach
the geese lifted off and were out of reach.
The geese flew far away and John hoped they would
return some day.

Next winter John was surprised to see Polly,
she came close to greet him and seemed very jolly.
John hurried home to tell his mother and Molly the good news
that once again Polly had returned to the shore.

Margaret Dawn Stratford

DONKEY EARS

'Why can't we all have donkey ears?'
The little girl did wail,
'And donkey fur, donkey feet
And a lovely donkey tail?'
'Don't you like being who you are?'
Replied the child's mother,
'For it would be boring
And confusing if we looked like one another.'
'But donkey ears are fluffy and cute
And they have such lovely feet.
I think to be a donkey
Would be rather neat.'
'No, my child, they make far too much noise
With that terrible, deafening bray,
And just what would you do with all your toys?
What kind of games would you play?'
'But Daddy says you drive him to drink,
He says you give him too much to do,
He doesn't have any time to think,
You call him an ass! That's a donkey too!'
'Child you sound more like your father
With every passing day,
I hope this silly notion of yours
Isn't here to stay!'
'Well perhaps I'm more like you then Mummy,'
She said after a while;
'For Daddy says you're stubborn as a mule,'
She retorted with a wicked smile!

Rebecca Osborne

THE STRANGER AND THE GNOME

'I'm lookin' for the crock o' gold,'
Said the stranger to the gnome.

'The croc o' gold yer say?' said the gnome,
Looking the stranger first up and then down.

'Yer much too old for the croc o' gold!'
'Too old!' repeated the stranger.
'Aye, that's right!' said the gnome -
'The croc o' gold is a fearsome creature!
So fierce he would doubtlessly eat yer!'

The stranger peered through nervous eyes.
'You mean croc-odile?' asked he.
'Mr Odile if yer please!' said the gnome.
'Yer really should show some respect.
Mr Odile is gold and not green -
The most wondrous creature yer ever have seen!
Except for his fillings - not gold they are green.'

'You don't understand,' said the stranger,
'The crock I seek is a pot filled with gold!'
'Why didn't yer say?' enquired the gnome,
'It was here yesterday, now it's been sold!'
'To whom?' asked the stranger, 'Who has it now?'
'Please tell me! My search is becoming a trial!'
The gnome cleared his throat and started to smile -
'I'm sorry - I sold it - to a Mr Odile!'

Philip J Mee

MEN FROM MARS

Playing football in the park?
They might be hiding behind that oak?
Oh, such tiny little folk
Men from Mars
When you go out in the dark
Looking up at all those twinkling stars
They're hiding behind
The garden shed
Could be men from Mars?

The village policeman
Loves his job,
Good old constable Bob.
'Are you sure sir?'
'You saw a flying saucer?'
'I will take a look
Just got to get out my book'
Oh no, those men from Mars!

Paul Wilkins

JACK FROST

In person he is never seen
Yet you know when he's been.
Some say he's a winter sprite
A fairy elf with impish delight.

With frozen pools on the ground
You see his work all around.
Winter icicles glisten and gleam
At freezing all, he's supreme.

But on frozen lakes danger hides
As children make their icy slides.
Ice so often weakened or thin
Can sudden a tragedy bring.

So avoid ponds that are deep
And to the icy puddles keep.
Enjoying all the winter delights
Or sledding and snowball fights.

Admire Jack's frosty patterns bold
As wintry landscapes unfold,
Sprinkled hoar frost along the trees
As fine white powder in the breeze.

Windowpanes all covered in rime
Etched with skilled traceries fine
And as those frosty fingers draw
Kids be safe, and know the score.

H D Hensman

THE VIKING

He was tall and bold,
His hair a mass of tangled gold.
Storm tossed, he came from afar,
Following his wandering star.

We crouched, watching
From cliff tops, fearing
The battles to come;
Some were struck quite dumb.

But one young girl, braver
Than the rest - our saviour
Though scarce thirteen years -
Ignored our fears.

Boldly she beckoned
That cruel man, invited
Him to eat with us
As our guest, then leave us.

Unharmed. Scarce breathing,
We waited, knowing
Our chances were slight.
Would he dine or fight?

Suddenly the Viking laughed,
Tossing his great gold head.
He was starving his gestures said;
So were his men, half dead.

That night our hall and streets rang.
Vikings boasted, maids sang.
By morning the longboat was gone,
And we were safe, everyone.

Pauline Kirk

WHEN FAIRIES COME

At the bottom of our garden there is a compost heap,
Which fairies visit every night, when I am fast asleep.
They play among the leaves and grass,
They dance among the weeds,
They blow on all the dandelions,
And scatter all the seeds.
They sing and dance, they laugh and shout
All through the long dark night.
And darting here, and darting there,
Like stars they shine so bright.
But when the night is ending,
Just before the break of day.
Giggling and laughing, they bid farewell,
And swiftly fly away.
And every night I lie awake, gazing at the compost heap,
But every night the fairies wait till I am fast asleep.

Linda Townend

BILL THE BLUEBOTTLE

There is a fly whose name is Bill,
He likes to sit by the windmill
And watch the sails go whirring by,
He wishes so fast he could fly.

But Bill is but a baby Blue,
His wings are small and only new
And he cannot yet fly so fast,
Not until his flying test is passed.

And so he waits until the day
The instructor asks him to pull away,
And with jellied nerves he flies his best
And flaps his wings with shaking legs.

One day he knows that he will fly
Up past the windmill's top so high,
And faster than the sails he'll go,
The fastest fly you'll ever know.

Helen Marshall

GRANDMA'S TALE

I was walking in the moonlight on yer grandad's arm,
We lived in the middle of nowhere; we owned this little farm.
Your grandad wanted romancin' - I was partial to his kiss,
But all of a sudden, things appeared a trifle amiss!
Right there above us, shone the brightest, bluest light.
I grabbed hold of yer grandad; he tried to calm my fright.
A huge, metallic silver disc, was coming in to land,
I wanted to run far away, grandad held me still by my hand.
The disc slowly twisted open, and completely shrouded by steam,
Came six little people, they were neither purple nor green!
People just like you - no more than this high,
Flying through time, in a disc in the sky.
They signalled their friendship, in an explosion of lights,
And then those six little aliens flew back into the night.

Claire Partridge

DO YOU WISH YOU'D A DOG LIKE BESS?

Do you wish you'd a dog like Bess,
Who listens when you talk,
Head on one side, with pleading gaze,
Just begging for a walk?

Her short black fur is velvety,
And soft and smooth to stroke
And, when you laugh, she runs about
As if to share the joke.

When in the park she meets her friends,
She bounds on happy paws.
'My ball!' you say, but no, it's hers,
It's clenched tight in her jaws.

Bess will not eat her bowl of meat
Until you've finished yours
And put some titbit in her dish,
Some veg or apple cores.

She'll then tuck in her little nose
And eat, and smack her lips,
Then to her water bowl she'll turn
And drink with dainty sips.

In cosy basket Bessie sleeps
But knows when you're awake,
She's always ready at the door
Her morning walk to take.

Do you wish you'd a dog like Bess?
She's small, but loyal, true,
And if you're very good I'll let
Her take a walk with you.

Margaret Drysdale

THE AMAZED OGRE

There was a big green ogre who lived in a swamp
in the thick of the forest.
He was 8 foot tall, with giant hands and feet and
huge bulging eyes.

He would roam about the forest, like a possessed
tiger, waiting for some villagers to prey upon and kill . . .

One day, he was roaming about as usual, hoping to
find some nice juicy villagers to eat, but to his
amazement he could not find any, not even a single one.
Feeling annoyed, he returned to his swamp hut,
and opening the door he let out a loud shriek!

Inside were all the village people held captured by 10 other ogres!
No wonder he couldn't find anything to eat!

Lorna Neave

A HALLOWE'EN NIGHT

Goblins, ghosts and Frankenstein,
Hallowe'en night gives you a fright . . .

Trick or treat,
Smell my feet,
Give me something good to eat.
A usual Hallowe'en night goes like this -

The bell goes . . . ding dong,
We open the door . . . out comes the song,
Dreading the time when we have to say.
Sorry, no sweets today,
Please go away.

The children moan and walk away.
Maybe you should've given them some pay.
When telling them 'Not tonight,'
Might turn into a gruesome fight.
With witches and warlocks,
And ghosts of many type.
You may end up with a bloody bite.

Claire Parker (12)

THERE WAS A LITTLE CHERUB

There was a little cherub, Kirsty was her name,
she had the face of an angel,
and blonde curly hair,
her lovely face did frame.
But she was a right wee demon,
when it came to chocolates, the same
for into that box, or packet
she would go and she did not stop,
until all had been eaten up, you know
she thought she might just get away with it, but even though
she did her best, the traces, not to show, it did not succeed.
For sure as sure, there was always a bit,
attached to her hair, for it went almost, everywhere.
Up would come the hand, to flick it back, I do declare,
And my! There's chocolate there, there and there!
One day she thought I won't be found out,
I shall cover my head with a bonnet, to keep it out
but she forgot, that if the box, was found empty
and her stomach let out a loud burp,
Guess who had to own up then,
this little cherub with no wings at all,
when, she called, 'Mummy, my tummy does hurt!'
A little cherub - yup!

M Lightbody

A Day Out

I met a young man from St Austell
He was only ten years old
Face covered with freckles
And hair of pure spun gold
Hiding of course.
As the train sped over the moors
Some magic he began to produce.
His thumb, disappeared, so did his head
A magician said I, when you are old
Not really, a vulcanoligist instead.

He mentioned great mountains, puffing and blowing
With big rings of smoke and lava just flowing
If you fall in you are dead.
His father is a police inspector
Two grandads, one saw a ghost,
Then along came big brother,
The one that gives you a poke
When the train came to a grinding halt,
They disappeared in a puff of smoke.

Mary Green

THE LONELY MONSTER

In the deep dark forest lurched a big grizzly monster,
so fierce, hideous and frightening,
the monster sometimes scared of its own reflection.

Huge bulging eyes, staring, following you everywhere.
No arms or legs, but it has two heads,
and webbed stubs with long sharp claws.

The monster lives alone in the forest,
only the trees to talk to,
as all the other animals are too scared,
they run away and hide.

'Would you be my friend?' he asks the trees,
but they don't reply, they seem to whisper to themselves,
the monster is so lonely and unhappy.

One day a young man, tall, strong and brave,
walks through the forest,
he's not scared of anything,
or so he says!

The monster hides in the trees,
excited about the prospect of a new friend,
he's not seen before in the forest.

The monster decides to play and shows itself,
the man jumps back and screams like a girl,
frozen, he cannot move, he's too scared.

The monster groans, trying to talk, but roars only louder,
the man just stands still.

The monster seems to like the man and decides to hug him.
Being a monster hug,
the man disappears.

The monster is sad again because he has no friends.

Kim Rands

A Magic Time

The upturned table was a pirate ship
we were the scourge of the sea
with my cutlass and my eyepatch
there was no one feared like me,
with a telescope to my one good eye
watching for land to come into view,
the skull and cross bones on our flag
from a stout table leg mast flew,
as we searched for buried treasure
this fearless captain and his crew.

The toys tea party for you and me
the food so delicious, the best we'd seen
with pretend cakes and pretend tea
to us it was a banquet fit for a queen
or armed with home-made helmet,
sword and shield, we became brave
knights as we sought out the dragon
and the covered table was its cave.

The one eyed teddy bear with a cap
perched on bandaged ears
was a great train driver sitting
at the front of a row of chairs,
whilst I punched holes in tickets
and you carried a bag for the fares.
Outside we'd be explorers in the
jungle looking for a rhinoceros
but next door's cat asleep in the
long grass was good enough for us.

Out of the dressing up box we
could be anything we wanted to be
no limit to our imagination, nor
inhibitions in this land of fantasy,
did we fulfil our dreams before
reality began and the fantasy end,
can we still share in the wonder
of a child's world of let's pretend?

Moon Stone

ALICE IN WONDERLAND

When Alice met the white rabbit
In that wonderland of dreams,
It must have been sheer magic,
For nothing was as it seems.
When storybook characters came to life
Must have appeared so funny and rare.
Playing their part
And meeting Alice with golden hair.
Who was invited or not.
To sit down at a table with a dormouse asleep
And trying to pour out from a huge teapot.
At the Madhatter's tea party - quite a treat.
Imagine playing Flamingo croquet with a queen so proud.
While the knaves painted roses, red
And being shouted at so loud
Fearing for their head.
Think of meeting a Cheshire cat
Grinning from ear to ear so.
It must have been an annoying fact,
That he used to come and go.
Oh all the strange adventures she did find,
Which grew more curious by the minute.
When she found a drink and cake with a sign,
Eat and drink me on it,
Which Alice could not resist to try,
So risky like oysters who dance upon the sand,
But never question why,
No wonder we love to read Alice in Wonderland.

M Hanmer

BOD

Bod the alien landed with a bump on Earth,
A smelly thing, he hadn't heard of surf,
His head went left his body went right,
He wondered if his trousers were too tight,
Hair stuck up like a big bunch of carrots,
Sitting on the top were two orange parrots.

Green sticky slime from his nose it did run,
We won't say what came out from his tum,
Stinky socks with holes covered his toes
A gas mask was needed to cover your nose,
Mouldy chewing gum stuck to his feet,
Spat from kid's mouths, when they walked the streets.

One day he burped so very, very loud,
People were amazed it drew a large crowd,
A child looked into his wide oval mouth,
In his belly was a telly the programme Due South,
He twiddled the knobs for a better view
Sausage and mash from his tummy he did spew.

Greedy thing was Bod's middle name,
Stuffing his face all day he had no shame.
Crisps, biscuits, sweets, breakfast, dinner, tea,
It went on and on for everyone to see,
His burping got louder as each day passed by,
Especially after eating three steak and kidney pies.

The time had come to say cheerio and goodbye
All his new friends he'd made began to cry
His adventure was over, it was time to go home
He wished he could remember where he'd put his comb
In his rocket he went up, up and away,
Oh dear sweet Bod, do please come back another day.

Ali Ashley

GRAVEYARD

Graveyards are eerie and mysterious
the dark fog makes me curious
dismal broken moss covered tomb
they scare me to my doom
I dream of running away
to the graveyard where dead things lay
I stop because I snagged my shirt
the more time I waste I sink into the dirt
sinking I am beginning to get worried
I shouldn't have stopped I should have hurried
a cry out of the dark behind me
the place is alive every grave, every tree,
I scream out in all my terror
but the more I scream the terror gets nearer
the darkness is closing in it's suffocating
I sink to my knees and now I'm shaking
I don't think I'm going to live through this
not going to grow older all the things I miss
eyes everywhere have come to take me back
something grabs me and drags me into the black
further away from the reality I know
now I suppose it was my time to go
but I haven't said goodbye yet
there are lots of people I haven't met
no! I'm not going to let them do this to me
so I struggle and get away I'm free
I look back and all I see
is the branch that I had snagged on the tree.

I stop once again I'm in a trance
I'm in my back garden standing on the plants
dreams do sometimes have meanings
they produce images, pictures and things
a dream like this could never come true
least that's what I think about you?
Sleep well tonight.

Jamie Barnes

A LLAMA NAMED LOUISE

A llama named Louise
Had very knobbly knees,
Chased into some trees
By a swarm of bees,
Sat to eat some peas
Caught a foot disease
Feet now smell of cheese!
Trees were blown by breeze,
Causing nose to sneeze
And her knees to freeze!

Gail

SOPHIE'S PARTY

At my party
there's jelly and custard
great big pork pies and sausage
with mustard, there's lettuce
and tomatoes and carrots like sticks,
there's loads of crisps
and sandwiches, built up like bricks,
there's cakes of all sizes some
round and some square,
and one on the sideboard
that's shaped like a chair
and one that has candles
ready to be lit.

At my party
there's balloons on the wall
and a big long banner
tied up in the hall,
that says Happy Birthday
and seven today.

At my party
we went into the garden
to play a few games
just mind the flowers,
and daddies cold frames,
we are all getting tired
it's been a long day
and to see all my friends
go, really was sad
but it's been the best
birthday, the best
that I've had.

John J Axon

A FAMILY CHAT BETWEEN TWO BACTRIAN CAMELS

Said Baby B to Mummy B 'I'm perplexed
to know just why
with all this lovely sunshine
and deep cerulean sky -
why I should be, as you are too,
encumbered by the fact
that two large humps of prodigious size
are carried on our backs?'
'Tis like your lovely lashes, dear
of long, uncommon size
which sweep and keep so well away
the sand from out your eyes -
and deep within the humps, my dear
where'ere in drought you scrabble
you've got your private wat'ring hole
for independent travel.
'But why, Mama, have *I* got feet
that make me wonder why -
they're quite so large, they really are -
they make me sigh and cry.'
'They're large, my dear, because you see
you'd sink up to your knees - in sand
if you had little piggy feet
or feet as wee as fleas.'
'I see, Mama, it all adds up.
There's little more to do,
but tell me, please
where *is* this sand -
we're in London zoo.'

Andrew A Duncan

DECISION TIME

Why do girls have to have brothers?
It seems so dreadfully unfair
You think you've got the place to yourself
When suddenly they are there.

They rush back from school with a clatter
And retire to the room next to mine,
They shout as though deaf to each other
And play loud CDs all the time.

They empty the packets of crisps
And search through the fridge for the coke
They've eaten the last of the biscuits
Well, what can you expect of a bloke!

I'm trying to do my homework
I've put cotton wool in my ears
But I can't exactly ignore them
As they rush up and down our stairs.

I've spoken about it to my mother
All she says is 'Boys will be boys.
I think you are exaggerating darling
I haven't noticed the noise.'

So I'm thinking of writing a notice
And carefully choosing each word
'Home wanted for sensible teenager
No other children preferred.'

Vivien Bayley

A MEMORY

When dad and I walked, hand in hand
Towards that dark and wooded land
Along the path, where elms still stand.

To remind me of that night, so mild.
And of that small fir growing wild
A Christmas tree for me, his child.

And the starry sky seemed set alight
With silver coins, all polished bright
With a velvet cloth - that special night.

John Rossiter

WONDERLAND

I stumbled once upon a tree, a tree that reached so high,
I could not see the top of it; it seemed to reach the sky!
I knocked three times upon this tree and waited for a while,
Then something amazing happened, which made me truly smile.
A door opened wide within the trunk, a little gnome appeared,
He was two feet tall, had a smiling face with a long and greying beard.
He waved me in and sat me down; we had a wonderful tea,
It was so much fun but then he said - he had more to show me.
He pushed a button and to my delight another door appeared,
Though I was having so much fun this all seemed pretty weird!
But anyway, through we went - and oh what a wonderful sight,
We'd entered a different place I think - the sun gave a pinkish light.
It was all so strange I stopped and stared, the trees did catch my eye,
For they had faces, and smiled at me - We waved as we walked by.
On we went, we reached a town - a town all full of Gnomes,
Busy shopping - it was market day, then back to their tree homes.
We went to a park, then round the shops, I made so many friends,
What an adventure I had that day, I didn't ever want it to end.
But when we got back my new friend asked if I'd come and visit again,
'Of course I will,' I said with glee - 'tomorrow morning at 10?'

Amanda Hall

CHILDREN

Children are infuriating
Passionately engaging
From year one to year dot
You certainly are not
Bored, but laughing or sad
That's the function of children
And that is that
To teach you about life
What you had not learned
Before this time
Life's complexity and
Whatever is 'that'
You have not learnt yet
Accepting the children
We will learn - hopefully
What is meant to be.

Marja von Ronkko

THE TIGER CAT

Once upon a time there was a little kitten,
Who grew into a fine big cat,
Looking more like a tiger every day,
So handsome as he lay on the blue mat.

When he was small,
Someone had thrown him over the high wall,
His mother had died in the ditch,
Probably trying to save him.

As cats don't talk like humans now,
We will never know how he met his fate,
As he grew his character did so too,
He was playful and wild, a bit like you,

If visitors came to tea,
He would disappear up the chimney out of sight,
It was just as well the fire was not lit,
He would stay there until everyone left at night.

A tree was growing near to the window,
On a summer's day the window would be open,
He would climb on to a branch,
All day he would sit as if in a trance.

Just waiting for a chance,
To pounce on any bird who was careless,
Pancakes, creamed rice and fish,
His favourite foods in a dish.

He pulled the dog's tail,
And made him wail,
But at night he would cuddle up tightly,
For warmth and comfort from the dog,
So perhaps he was not so dim,
As he would have us believe of him.

Mary Lawson

HAROLD - THE VERY SUPERIOR TURTLE

Harold the turtle was as haughty as could be,
Few creatures were on the same social level as he,
Fish were rather common and frogs were just the same,
And as for slithering snakes, they really were mundane.

Birds were always flighty and ready to take wing,
They never chose to listen, they only chose to sing,
Mammals too, hot blooded and otters amongst the worst,
They made him so indignant he felt that he would burst!

Humans he could not stand, the worst of all the lot!
As babies making silly noises in a pram or carrycot!
As adults on a beach, trying to get a tan
And end up looking like sausages sizzling in a pan!

No, to be a turtle was simply the very best,
Showing off your social skills and puffing out your chest.
Talking to other turtles who know what you were all about,
Instead of conversing with centipedes or socially inferior trout.

Oh, to be a turtle and converse with others of your kin,
To discover who was out of fashion and who of course was in.
Mix only with turtles was old Harold's sage advice
And never talk to lower classes like cats and dogs and mice!

Keith Davies

A MARKET DAY

Such a beautiful welcome the flowers gave, a gesture I
returned with a friendly wave, as I entered this world
of make believe,
to see so many people in one little place, and wherever
I looked a friendly face,
then my spirits were lifted even more, as I tasted this
feast of bargains galore,
baskets with such a beautiful weave, hand crafted too I
would believe, jewellery spread out all nice and gleaming,
old man on bench quietly dreaming, clothes with colour
you couldn't imagine, cabbage, carrot, apple, and pear, ugly
antiques all handled with care, stall holders shouting
above noise to be heard, old woman handling a well plucked bird,
church tower stark against sky turning grey, bell in clock
tower calling the day,
but too soon came the time for me to go, and with a backward
glance that would know, that my eyes had not my mind
deceived, I left this little world of make believe, and
promised myself I would again come down, to this old
market place, in this old market town.

Jim Cuthbert

MY FUNNY MAN

I know a funny man
He would drive a funny car to work
To feed his funny coo's.

He would run his funny tractor
With funny music playing
Funny curls popping out under his cap.

He would pull me funny faces
We would roar with funny laughter
Every funny day.

Funny when mud would splat
A funny welly with a hole
A funny rip in a boilersuit.

Finally the funny coo's had some grub
We'd change into our funny clean shoes
All ready for our funny home.

A funny flask o tea
A funny wee sarnie tae eat
For my funny, funny daddy
And his funny wee lass.

Stacey Tully

TOY STORY

You had a friend that was always there
Then someone came along and made it unfair
You were Andy's favourite cowboy
Now it's a spaceman and you tell him he's a toy
All your friends like him now while you can't understand
And you don't know how.

On your foot 'Andy' is in crayon
On his it is marker, which is better by a tonne
Little Bo Peep likes him better too
So you have to find out what to do
You knocked him out of the window because he was your only foe
Andy saved your pullstring by taking you away
Buzz found you and you're lost at the petrol station to stay.

When Andy got home he had realised you were gone
He had no clue what was going to be done
You tried to get home to say your goodbye bid
But the others thought you were sad
Not to mention that Buzz went mad.

You told him to pull himself together
And when the sun came it was perfect weather
You're the Sheriff and you can't let people down
Buzz's expression changed to a smile from a frown.

With work of two friends you got RC to help you
Now you knew exactly what to do
Off you shot down the road
To the air you flew but dropped RC to the load.

You made your landing safely in the back of the car
Where you were glad to be by far.

Zoe Thompson

THE E.TS' ELECTION

When you walk back to the car today
You're sure of a big surprise,
When you walk back to the car today,
You will not believe your eyes!

For all E.Ts from miles around
Have gathered here, on our football ground,
Today's the day they hope to choose a new leader.

They do not speak, but will cast their votes
By making their mark, then pass their notes
Which show their choice, and soon they'll have a new leader.

Jo Brookes

GROWING UP

Growing up, is not too easy,
Maturing too, can be a bore,
Rules are made, and can be broken,
Keeping them, you surely score.
A pleasant smile, a cheery word,
Will cost you, not a penny,
A helping hand, when one is down,
And friends, you will have many.
Mum needs a hand, that table to clear,
Dad needs some help, the grass to shear,
A nice cup of tea, when things get tough,
When one can see, one has had enough,
You'll have a warm glow, at the end of the day,
For each good turn, you have done on the way.
Don't look for reward, when doing good,
Your character, you are forming.
Just say a prayer, when you get up,
For guidance, every morning.

Sarah Beere

SNAGIRILLORANG - HIPPHORFLAM DUCK

A head just like a snake.
A neck like a giraffe.
A body you could die for!
Or one to make you laugh?

A chest like a gorilla.
Arms like orangutangs.
It turns its head and gazes.
Watch out for those sharp fangs!

A bottom like a hippo.
A tail just like a horse.
You'd like to know its name.
You would, of course, of course.

Legs like a pink flamingo
And webbed feet like a duck.
Entered a beauty contest
But soon ran out of luck.

If you should see this creature,
Be sure to ask its name,
It couldn't be more simple,
Will you join in my game?

A snagirillorang
Hyphen hipphorflam duck
Who likes to eat your children
Then roll round in the muck.

But, don't go having nightmares,
You won't see it appear
Unless you stay indoors all day
And always live in fear.

So out you go and find a friend,
Life will begin, your fear will end.

Catherine Craft

THE DREAM CATCHER

At the dead of night
The dream catcher
Wanders your room
Hush, hush little one
Your boy is not asleep yet
Just close your eyes
Squeeze them tight
Close the shutters
And say goodnight.

Come in enter my dream
I have just got to the best part
My baby brother is in the bath,
Mother is paying the milkman,
Dad is watching Star Trek on the TV
And I'm playing with my megadrive
And winning of course.

When water comes splashing down
Quick as a flash I run up the stairs
Struggle through the water,
Save my brother,
While dad is swimming for his life
And mother says
Your dream catcher is very brave.

Kate Davies

IN THE GRAND SCHEME

Caterpillar and worm could not agree
If they belonged to the same family
Caterpillar said 'You are so thin and I am so fat
And as you can see there's no doubt in that.

I am so pretty and you are so plain
To be like you leaves nothing to gain
One day I will sleep and when I awake
I shall then a butterfly make.

But look at you, you're long and all brown
As dull as can be and will always be round
But I will have wings of a beautiful hue
How can you *think* that *I* am like *you.*'

The worm at first was hurt and all sad
The thought of a cousin had made him quite glad
But then he said 'No, I'm not like you
For you are conceited thro and all thro.

I can dig deep right down in the earth
The farmers and gardeners know of my worth
Without my ploughing the soil all the time
Plants would just die with no air to survive.

I help the fishermen catch the best fish
So they can eat a good tasty dish
The birds of the air eat me this is true
So with my help, their song we won't lose.

It is well known Mother Nature needs me
The circle of life will always be
But once *you* have laid your first batch of eggs
Then it's all over you'll soon be dead.

So now you know your part is so small
And in the grand scheme . . . the worm has it all.'

Gillian Mullett

THE GHOST

Soft, cool, misty fog,
Swifting oozily over my bed
Sending ice chilling winds
Down my spine,
Eye of charcoal,
Mouth of darkness
An expressionless face,
Glaring at me,
A hovering body,
With no arms or legs,
Moving swiftly and steadily,
Brightening up every inch
Never failing to terrorise.

Lizzi Giles

GARGOYLE

In the darkest corner of the highest chamber room,
It sometimes came to squat and watch
The sanguine way she moved.
It was an evil presence, maybe just an essence
Of a life perhaps extinguished in the flesh.
Yet, she could feel its gaze
And she knew it knew her ways,
So she had learned to tolerate her ill-intentioned guest.

It had never been malicious
And yet, she felt it could be vicious
To a lover unsuspecting in her upper chamber room.
It was an evil presence
And could soon exude a menace
As it squatted out of line of sight
In the corner's twilight gloom.

It gave the vague impression
Of a Goblin or a Gargoyle
Though its structure was uncertain,
Just a shadow on the wall.
But it would never leave her,
Obsessed to oversee her.
Perhaps it wished to be her,
But she knew it was inside there as she stood out in the hall.

She could feel its presence pulling her,
Willing her to go inside,
So it could feed on watching her
Where she could find no place to hide
From the paranormal parasite
With so insatiable an appetite,
A lust or a perversion to eat away her pride.

But then one early summer night
When honeysuckle filled the air,
A quiet foot-fall struck the stair by fading sunset light.
A secret suitor approached with stealth
To place a rose upon the shelf
Above her dressing table and in direct line of sight.

He hoped that she would see it there
When she returned from breaking bread
With her beloved brother and his wife.
But as she climbed the tower tall
Unto the highest chamber room,
She could feel impending doom,
A smell of bleeding in the gloom,
The seeping of a life.

On opening the chamber door,
A trail of droplets on the floor led to a blood-red rose.
It lay there in a shadowed place,
A thorn the source of blood-red gore.
And, although she got to wondering,
The suitor came no more.

John Tirebuck

HEY SANTA DON'T FORGET

To Santa I send this letter
As I've been a naughty boy
I promise I'll do better
If you bring me lots of toys.

Mammy says I won't get any
As I've not been good at all
And I don't deserve a present
I've just driven her up the wall.

Santa do make sure
That you bring the toys I want
Or I'll kick Rudolph up his bum
And give your sleigh a shunt.

Yes Santa I'm the naughtiest boy
That you have ever met
Just make sure you bring the toys
Hey Santa don't forget.

Marie Horridge

THE SCARY DRAGON

One day as I was walking along
I could feel there was something wrong.
I looked in the hedge and then I could see,
Two big beady eyes looking at me.

Should I calmly walk by or run back home,
What does it look like, could it be a gnome?
But then a loud noise came from behind the parked wagon,
Oh my goodness me, it was a huge, big dragon.

I started to run back to my house,
Well it's definitely bigger than a mouse.
Well boys and girls what should I do?
I just hope there's only one and not two.

Do you think I should catch him with this wire?
But as I get near to the dragon it suddenly breathes out fire.
It all seemed so hot and bright,
It just gave me a huge fright.

As I fell down onto the ground,
I could hear this funny sound,
Then screams and shouts had woken me up,
Then I see Sammy my little pup.

He was jumping around and licking my face,
Steady on Sammy give me some space,
I heard the door open and the children come in,
Then I realised that I must have been dreaming.

Kathy Buckley

VERY STRANGE (NURSERY RHYMES)

Little Miss Muffet wasn't on her tuffet,
She was settled here to stay,
What it said in the rhyme hadn't happened,
The spider hadn't frightened her away.
Little Jack Horner wasn't in his corner,
He was sharing his rich plum pie,
Now he really deserves what the rhyme says,
'What a good boy am I.'
Humpty Dumpty wasn't on the wall,
He was rubbing his sore broken head,
But we all knew he had a lucky escape,
We thought when picked up, he'd be dead.
Little Bo Peep had got tired of the sheep
And had come to join the rest,
She didn't care if they never came home,
She was dressed in her Sunday best.
Little Red Riding Hood hadn't gone to the wood,
So she's now quite well and hearty,
They are all to share grandma's goodies,
And it makes it a wonderful party.
Little Tommy Tucker needn't sing for his supper,
He's going to get it for free,
He's happy enough to join all his friends,
When they tuck in this mouth watering tea.

Georgie Porgy pudding and pie,
Won't kiss the girls and make them cry,
He'll be very busy with party games,
So time will soon pass by,
Mary, Mary quite contrary,
Has joined the others as well,
Sitting down with these famous folks,
What a lovely tale she could tell.
All the nursery rhymers in a reunion,
A great get together for all,
The next time they will be more ambitious,
They will have a grand gala and ball.

Edith Antrobus

MOUNTAIN BIKING

Racing round the forest track
With not a thought of getting back.
The sun went down, my mates went home,
I cycled round then on my own.
Then something gave, I lost my grip and
Landed in a twisted heap.
Rubbing my head and looking around . . .
I thought I heard the strangest sound, like
A cackle from a witches clack,
Creeping through the forest black.
So I pushed my bike and undertook
To walk a way and take a look.
Just over there as I was nearing,
I saw a hovel, in the clearing . . . and
High above a door ajar,
Did arc across a shooting star and higher still
Three flying brooms . . .
Were dancing with a shining moon.
Then . . . stirring gruel as black as night,
Three shadows in the firelight.
Tricky mushrooms strew the floor and
Little bits of lizard jaw,
With a path outside all made of bones,
Cast out, by these talloned crones . . .
Differing kind of stinky herb now.
Glowing at its hissing curb!
I'd walked about a mile I'd say,
My clothes and head in disarray,
Deciding not to ask assistance . . .
I crept away into the distance.
'Stay with your mates' was best I knew,
I could have wound up in a stew!

Roger Mosedale

DREAMS AND DARES

Timothy George went up the stairs
Sleepy and tired with his teddy bear.
Closing his eyes his prayers he said
As he knelt with his teddy beside the bed.

Through the window the bright moon peeped,
As two little friends fell fast asleep.
Biscuits and chocolate they'd shared in the nursery,
As they told of the fun they had had with Marjory.

She Minniehaha; he Hiawatha,
They had played all day with Henry and Arthur.
Mountains they had climbed and rivers they had crossed,
Then deep in the forest they nearly were lost,
But plans are made;
And dreams will be shared,
When they meet tomorrow,
And brave feats are dared.

Joan Thompson

CECIL AND PAM

Two little frogs named Cecil and Pam,
Sat lazily by the pool
The rain was falling lightly
It was perfect for making a fool
Of Jeremy cat who was frightened of frogs
And hated it when they hopped
'Here he comes' said Cecil and Pam
As out of the house he popped.

Jeremy never noticed the frogs
As he sauntered past the pond
Then Cecil and Pam did their highest hop
Of this they were quite fond
Poor Jeremy leap ten foot high
And howled with dreaded fear
He landed on top of a gooseberry bush
Then back to the house *oh dear.*
The two little frogs laughed with glee
What an adventure they'd had today
'It must be teatime' Cecil said,
As they merrily hopped away.

Jacqui Wykes

DONALD AND THE UNICORN

Donald-Comes-Running is his real name,
But he is known as Donald by his master
And portrayed as a puppet of his better self
In an enchanted forest without compare.

Donald lives with his grandmother
As all his other kin are dead
And he searches for a miracle to cure
His grandma of his master's curse.

Never before had an answer so been born
It surely was a sign from God
Donald fondled the goat with one straight horn
And tied a string around his neck.

From the woods by the field of corn
There came a distant shout:
'It's a unicorn! It's a unicorn!'
Came the echo as he ran.

Straight to his grandma at the tailor's shop
He entered and showed his find
'It's a unicorn!' he panted to Pop
'A real, live, wonderful miracle.'

'And how do you propose to do that?'
His sceptical grandmother asked
'With God's help and talking cure
The tailor answered, kneeling beside the kid.

And so it came about
Donald's master lifted his curse,
Let fall the strings, restored her faith
And, with an angel, completed the cure.

Rosemary Smith

A MEAL WITHOUT INTERESTING FOOD
IS LIKE FEEDING ON GRASS
(Indian Proverb)

Every morning up to the fence
There comes a sheep, but has she sense
As she keeps the birds in great suspense?
Such a crafty sheep is she.

Finding scraps from the house is in her mind.
She eats them all, leaves none behind,
So there's nothing left for the birds to find.
A greedy sheep is she.

She stands there eating every day
Edibles from indoors thrown away.
So bad luck for magpie, crow and jay.
Not a sharing sheep is she.

Grass, she thinks is just a bore.
Cake and bread crusts are not raw,
For cooked food to her is something more,
A gourmet of a sheep is she.

She has no interest in 'sell by' date,
And she does not worry about her weight
While she has tasty food to masticate,
A one-track minded sheep is she.

She's left her flock up on the hill
And won't return till she's had her fill.
She certainly has the strongest will.
A determined sheep is she.

Then she ambles off to the high hedgerow
Where succulent flowers and nettles grow,
But such plants she does not wish to know.
A disdainful sheep is she.

Soon, her flock will be moved to pastures new.
No more tit-bits for her to chew.
So, she'll have to slim - a good thing too,
Then a healthy sheep she'll be.

Loré Föst

BRAIN DAMAGE

I had a little brain cell
But nothing did it know
And so I planted knowledge seeds
And watched them grow and grow
And when the crop had ripened
I harvested the grain
And stored away the new knowledge
Right here inside my brain.

But when I came to use it
The seeds had gone astray
Genetically modified
With canine DNA.
So now I've watered every tree
Down at the local park
I can't explain my actions now
For I can only bark.

So now I like to run around
And play in every ditch
My love life isn't what it was
I love the silly bitch.
My hair now grows all over me
In little curly tufts
And next year I am certain that
I'll win top prize at Crufts.

Mick Bull

TOMMY TUCKER

This is the tale of Tommy Tucker
Who used to have to sing for his supper
But now he's into frying and cooking
And each day gets more good looking
He tries to keep the girls at bay
But found his feet were made of clay
So no matter how he tried
From the girlies he could not hide
So he decided to play their game
And gave up cooking and thoughts of fame
And became instead an ordinary lad
Who nightly entertains girls at his pad.

June Clare

HOW DOES YOUR GARDEN GROW

Katie Dewdrop
Glistened deep
Within the petals
Of sweet rose
Awakened a face
A tender pink
That delicately grows

Rose thanking Dewdrop
Blessed the night
Welcomed morn
God's gift of light.

Irene Gunnion

EDWARD BEAR

He sits erect and upright
In a very large armchair.
He's a proud and clever fellow
With his nose up in the air.

His real name is Edward,
I always call him Ted
And always make him say his prayers
Before he goes to bed.

I take him everywhere I go
And he never will complain
So when I've nothing else to do
I take him there again.

Joyce Walker

A TALE FOR DAVI

'Don't eat all your chocolate eggs today!'
Young Davi's mum was heard to say.
'I think you should eat only one,
Or suffer nasty pains inside your tum!'

'I'll be a good boy!' beamed wee Davi -
Already covered in chocolate gravy!
Munch! Crunch! Munch! Crunch! He ate more chocci
Then his tum felt rumble-tumble-rocky!
He was sick! 'Mum, Dad, I feel quite ill!'

'Lucky lad - you don't need pills!'
Said his doctor/daddy who shook his head
'Though Davi - you must rest in bed!
No more sweets - lots of drinks!
What a boy! You *are* a minx!'

Davi Herbert awoke next day
He felt really well! Hip! Hip! Hooray!

The moral of this little tale is -
If you don't wish to end up sick 'n' pale
Do *not* eat all your eggs on Easter Sunday!
Spread them over several days
Then you can enjoy the holidays.

Patricia Cairns Laird

MRS WITCHES

Myles, Guy and Heather I hope you don't mind.
Would you take Nan some cakes, it would be so kind.
So off you go, now don't be slow for it's Hallowe'en
and you have far to go.
Swish! What's that? What a fright,
two scary witches flying through the night.
Nan's at last what a relief, these Hallowe'en antics
are beyond belief.
Nan says it's not witches we have seen,
only Mrs Brown and Mrs Green
who always go flying every Hallowe'en.
They are due to land and it would be grand
to go to their homes trick and treating.
Come taste our stew it's a lovely brew,
so soon they were happily eating.
The jet black cats watched it all
as they sat from wall to wall.
The very full three gratefully thanked
the two ladies for tea.
Soon homeward bound with their feet
barely touching the ground.
Their heads full of all they have seen.
So if perchance on Hallowe'en
two ghostly shapes can be seen.
Remember it's only Mrs Brown and Mrs Green.

Valerie Dee

MEG AND THE RED BALL

One day I heard some breaking glass
And I heard our neighbour yell
But exactly what the matter was
I couldn't really tell.

Then Mr Jones looked over the fence
'Is this your ball?' he said,
'It broke my kitchen window
And hit me on the head!'

'Excuse me, Mr Jones,' I said,
'My ball is soft and green.
That ball which you are holding
Is one I've never seen.

I really think that hard, red ball
Is meant for playing cricket
And as for breaking windows -
Well, I wouldn't be so wicked!'

Just then two boys arrived
To see what they could see
And Mr Jones was very cross
So I went in to tea.

Hugh Edwards

IT'S TRUE

A sofa filled with children
All crunched and not at ease
The video recorder was playing
And their noises were such a screech
The demon was their heart beater
For their adrenaline was rocket high.
Bedtime had now passed
Their eyes they couldn't close
For the demon was on a rampage
In their tiny minds.

Carolie Pemberton

WHO WANTS A KITTEN?

Kittens in the kitchen,
kittens on the stairs,
kittens on the landing
falling off chairs.

Kittens on the window ledge,
kittens in the loo.
We can't move for kittens
what are we going to do?

Here's a black and white one
sloshing in the jelly.
Where's the smudgy-nosed one?
Stuck behind the telly.

Kittens on the work-top,
kittens in the pan,
kittens in the bathtub
climbing on Gran.

If you need a kitten,
this is what you do:
come and knock on our door
and take one home. Or two.

Pat Mitchell

FREDERICK

Frederick was a crocodile,
With great big shiny teeth,
He had a hard and knobbly back,
But his tummy was smooth as silk,

Now Frederick he looked fearsome,
Although he was really quite kind,
He might look like he'd eat you for dinner,
But he always changed his mind.

With great big hands and great big feet,
He had claws that could tear you apart,
But Frederick wasn't that kind of croc!
He just didn't have the heart.

For Frederick was a gentle soul,
Who wouldn't harm a fly,
So remember, not everything is as it seems,
When you first meet - eye to eye . . .

Charmaine S Dawson

A Fairy Tale

Pearl is called Pearl because she scatters pearls of dew
Early morning and Posy helps the flowers to wake
Some need their faces washed like you
Pearl flits round with her magical cake

This attracts the bees, they love to appear
To gather nectar for honey flying many a mile
The cake is magic it contains sunbeams' rays to endear
When you set eyes on them it causes a smile

The fairies often get their wings torn by the rose's thorn
They help each other soon they are back on keel
Well and happy they recover, are not so worn
Then a lovely feast of petals make their meal

Suddenly their enemy appears on the local scene
Gobbly the goblin ready to cause trouble around
He nibbles the flowers, you can soon see where he's been
Causing havoc in the garden until he's found

'Ha ha I've caught you now you're in my trap'
Says Pearl, 'You cannot escape no way out'
Posy joins in with magic scissors snip snap
Gobbly goblin begins to scream and shout

With such a coward in their magic grasps
No quarter do they give, you will have to go away
'Please release me I'll be good I promise' Gobbly gasps
'Tonight you will be sentenced quickly, straight away.'
Fairy land was busy, a trial before the throne
Gobbly was sent far away, how he did groan.

Bessie Groves

PLAYTIME UNDECIDED

Shall we go out and play today
Or shall we stay in and play shops
Do you think Mummy will say we may
Or shall we play 'Top of the Pops'
Shall I be Mum, will you be Dad
Oh! dear, how perfectly mad
I'm a girl and so are you
Oh dear! What shall we do
Shall we go upstairs to play
Or shall we play on the stairs
Shall we play houses, or shall it be trains
Oh! Come on, let's go out before it rains
Oh come on, let's go out do
We can dig up the garden
Build a great dam
Rock the baby in the pram
Oh! What shall we do today
Oh come on, let's go out to play.

M Gurney

WIGGIN

*(Wiggin - Celtic fairy name for a cat prone to mishaps
and lacking in the usual feline skills)*

Alice found Wiggin one frosty morning
He was frozen and much worse for wear
But Alice had read that black cats were magic
And Wiggin was too hungry to care.

Everyone called Alice a bookworm.
She liked magic spell books the best,
But while Wiggin was happy chasing butterflies
Alice was planning his very first test.

To guarantee the spell was successful
She needed to collect everything that was listed.
Bristles snipped from Grandpa's moustache while he snoozed,
A black cat's whisker and a mouse's tail that was twisted.

Now poor Wiggin was not a skilled hunter.
Alice instructed him to find the correct prey,
But as he crouched and pounced headlong into things,
It became clear that it just wasn't his day.

Alice was to say the very least disappointed,
As her collection was not going well.
'Oh, I nearly forgot' she cried, yanking a large whisker,
Causing poor Wiggin to let out a piercing *'Miaow!'*

That night as moonlight shone around them,
Alice began reciting the very long spell.
Wiggin looked on as she mixed bits of moustache and his whisker
In a dish; with the slime from a snail.

In the morning they found to their horror
That the spell Alice had chose,
Although supposed to remove all her freckles
Had in fact left Grandpa with a huge boil on the end of his nose.

Karen Baseden

NANA

What it is like to be a nan?
I'll tell you my friend, if I can,
To gaze upon his big blue eyes,
His golden hair, his chubby thighs,
His sturdy legs and hands that grab
Whenever he can his nana's bag.
A puzzled look at flies and bees
To kiss all better his grazed knees.
To watch him dance and stamp his feet
A big smile when he gets a treat.
To watch him play and sing along
As we try to teach him a new song.
But best is tiny hands around my neck
To get a cuddle and a peck.
There is a God now I can say
Because he sent him down our way.
A little miracle, now quite grown
Knows what he wants, a mind of his own.
No-one on earth is as lucky as me
Because I'm Nan to our Robbie.

Linda Ross

BABY TROUBLE

Daddy, Daddy tell me why
Does our baby always cry?
Because he's hungry now my son,
I think I'd better fetch your mum.

Daddy, Daddy tell me why
Does our baby *still* cry and cry?
Because his nappy's wet my son
He wants a dry one on his bum,
I think I'd better fetch your mum.

Oh! Daddy now his cry keeps me awake in bed
Even though I suck my thumb and cuddle Ted
Come here son, climb upon my knee
Then I will rock and sing to just us three.

Jacqueline Taylor

SMOKE

I once had a rabbit called Smoke,
Who drank a whole can of Coke,
He drank far too much
And blew up his hutch
And no longer thought it a joke.

E Osmond

CATERPILLARS' PARTY

Ben said, 'Right let's all meet at Mrs Jones' gate,'
'Okay,' said Millie, 'at about quarter to eight.'
'I will bring a big cabbage leaf,' said Ben, 'to eat,'
Then Millie said, 'and some nectar please, it tastes sweet.'

And so the scene was set for this little party,
The guests were caterpillars, not people you see,
There'd be various colours and sizes about,
Different textures and with hairy ones no doubt.

News of the caterpillar do soon got spread around,
Creating excitement above and below ground.
Day arrived, caterpillars close to the gate sprawled,
'Come, let us in,' cried Millie, 'Let's have a ball.'

A party, what a splendid idea, I must say,
When all the smart caterpillars came out to play.
When with relish the large cabbage leaf was devoured
And much nectar was drunk from large cup shaped flowers.

S Mullinger

THEE OLD LADY OF GLOOM

A haggard old lady shows her gloom
Sweeps so frantically with willow wood broom.
Hides her face behind see-through veils,
Has poison ivy for rings, with purple painted nails.

Cleans in and out of children's toys,
Then locks away all their playtime joys.
Voices her opinion with grumbling moans,
Spells out a concoction of casting groans.

Mangle for squeezing goblins' tongues,
As howling wolves sing their songs
Pixies' ears, crocodile tears,
Hyenas laughing hear their sneers.

Cave of bats and dragons' teeth,
Dispel any happiness, shower with grief.
Run away from cast off stitches, knit one,
Pearl one sees the gathering of witches.

Too many cooks spoil the broth
And all the witches begin to cough.
Groans and moans under a smiling moon,
Who laughs away thee old lady of gloom.

John Holloway

HIGHER AUTHORITY

A little green man came to tea,
I felt nervous, as nervous could be;
But he said, 'Don't be fright,
Everything is alright;
They've just sent me down to see,
What on earth is going on here?
Still plenty of troubles I fear,
Well, I'm from on high,
Way up in the sky
And I trouble-shoot all through the year.
Your problems I can speedily end,
On that you can surely depend,
We are so superior you see;
After all, I am visiting you,
But you cannot come up to see me!'

Vera Sykes

TRIP-TRAP

I am crouching in dry shadows
I am waiting
lying here for you

my coat is like Africa
can you see me?
I am hidden from your eyes

I am a shaggy bundle of energy
sprawling in water
eyes just visible

I sing when moon pours
silver over water,
slave of darkness

owls fly onwards on silent wings
I listen, I hear
wing beats. My pelt

is silvered. I am invisible
in your eyes
which seem blind

Trip-trap, trip-trap.

Waiting, Can you see me?
My weapon is sheathed
I leave your bones to wind

T Webster

THE INSECTS

I am a wriggly wiggly worm,
Hardly anyone likes me,
Except of course the birds and fish,
They like me for their tea.

I am a spider weaving my web,
I catch the flies who come into my bed.
People don't like me, but I mean them no harm,
If they try to catch me, I run with alarm.

I am a beetle, hard, black and shiny,
I crawl along everywhere that's very grimy.
I am a slug, no-one likes me,
Because I eat all their plants for my dinner you see.

I am an ant, busy all day,
Running around every which way.
I and my friends never rest until,
We have built our house, called an ant hill.

I am a bee, buzzing all around,
Collecting nectar from flowers, all that can be found.
I live in a hive, like the day to be sunny,
The queen bee ensures we make the honey.

I am a butterfly, so beautiful that's me,
I like to fly, fly and be free.
When I come to rest, so my beauty you can see,
Please never, never try to catch me.

Maud Eleanor Hobbs

THE MOUSE AND THE SPIDER

The little mouse liked inspecting the clock
And thinking it similar, the cuckoo he'd mock.
He'd run up and peer out as the clock struck one,
Then run down again, it was such great fun.
Unlike the mouse, the spider no enjoyment did get,
As he climbed up the spout to get out of the wet,
He climbed to the top to see sunshine at last,
But always got there as a cloud went past.
Then down would come raindrops to spoil all his fun
And Incy found he was back again where he'd begun.

Jean C Pease

THE CHIMNEY SWEEP'S BOY

Like silent, drab wraiths we all creep
Round the legs of John, head chimney sweep;
Awakened by him in the harsh, chill morn,
Better by far we had never been born.

'Master!' I whimper 'Oh, please let me sleep.
The straw is dirty, but the dream was deep.
I cannot face more of the smell and grime
In chimneys that hold me locked in black time.'

'Young varmint!' roars John striking my back,
'A damn good thumping is what you lack.
I've been so good, now you shall feel the whip!
Or I'll break your neck in my mighty grip.'

A terrified shadow, hazily black,
I run from John's anger, his pitiless whack.
I pray God I'll die in the dark upright tomb.
Will it be like going back to the womb?

Joan Kelly

Untitled

Dirty, smelly cars rusting everywhere,
People behind the steering wheel driving without a care.
Polluting the environment that's what they are doing,
Driving through the countryside, no more cows are mooing.
No more birds chirping high in the sky,
Pollution, pollution, why oh why oh why.
We should all take care of the things around,
From little birds that fly to slimy worms deep within the ground.
Cos one day you know if we're not careful things will be gone,
Then people will be thinking to themselves, where did we go wrong.

Shane Weeks-Pearson

IN MY BOX

In my box I shall put the whisper of the sea
And the spring of a Jack-in-a-box
Or the ink of coloured felt tip pens

In my box I shall put the most beautiful shell in the sea
And the wrapper of a chocolate
Or the tail of a sugar mouse

In my box I shall put the feathers of a pillow
And the fur of a cat
Or the cleverness of a scientist

In my box I shall put the darkness of a cave
And the pollen of the flower
Or the goldness of the sun.

Caroline Watson (10)

MONSTER 2

I'm back, I'm hungrier for you
I'll eat a whole human or even two,
I hunt for dinner and live in a cave
I enjoy parties and like a good rave!
I'll attack my victims outside a club
I'm as 'ard as nails and can swim like a sub
Where you hear bones crunching I'm munching
I'm coming your way so don't, don't even say
What a terrible beast I am.

Mark Page

HARRY POTTER

J K Rowling a talented author
Wrote a book about a boy called Harry Potter.
He did not know he was a wizard
He went to Hogarts where there were lots of lizards.
He had messy black hair
His aunt kept cutting it and that wasn't fair.
He had green eyes and a lightning bolt scar
And every wizard that saw him thought he was a star.
James and Lily were his mum and dad
When they died it was very sad.
That's all about Harry Potter
Created by J K Rowling, an excellent author.

Niarah Ahmed (11)

OFF ON HOLIDAY

Flying up in the sky
In an aeroplane so high
I'm getting away today,
Going off on holiday

So far out of reach
Lazing on the beach
Fun in the sun
Has only just begun

In the pool it's even better
Except a little wetter
I'm glad I got away today
I'm glad I'm off on holiday.

Karen McGachy (13)

A WORLD FOR THE FUTURE

A world for the future would be great,
There's nothing really that I'd hate
All the time I'd eat chocolate every day
But when I didn't I'd just play.
Roses and tulips would all be the same
And all the lions would be tame.
Under a rainbow there will be gold in a pot,
If you touched it you'd be as small as a spot.
Out come the pixies when it's time to play,
Out they would come for a day.
All the time you could fly a kite
Even in the cold, gloomy night.

Zoe-May Hassall (10)

UNTITLED

Hearts and flowers
with golden showers
until the day is done
to see and be with my friends
and then have some great fun.

Hearts and flowers
with golden showers
until the day is done
to laugh, to cry
to stroll on by
throughout the stars have shone.

Hayley Pollard (12)

MEMORANDA

Once upon a lunchtime, there lived a fair secretary named Memoranda. She had long silken tresses the colour of toner cartridge ink and skin as creamy-white as correction fluid. She was honest, kind and dreamy and always fed the pigeons on her way to work. But it was her misfortune to be imprisoned by a firm of enchanted accountants, where she toiled ogrish hours for very little pay. She also had trouble with wolves.

One day, fair Memoranda was about to flee her grim workstation to meet her godmother for lunch, when she accidentally pricked her finger on a paper clip and fell into a deep, caffeine-free sleep.

She slumbered peacefully for a hundred minutes. If her flinty boss had found her, poor Memoranda would've been transported back to the beastly realm of secretarial agencies from whence, as if by magic, she'd appeared. Suddenly from nowhere, astride his charger-cum-moped, arrived young Lee, the bead-toting, goatee-sporting, hairy courier.

Upon beholding Memoranda slumped gracefully across her keypad, Lee was so beguiled he delivered himself unto her instead. Kissing her upon the brow, he roused her from her office stupor and of course she fell in love with her prince. Together, they tripped merrily hand in hand to his waiting charger-cum-moped, on which they sped into the midday haze to the land of Newquay, where her knight errant surfed on occasional weekends.

Memoranda, as far as I know, lived with hippie Lee ever after.

Jonathan Goodwin

SPIDER'S END

It was a warm sunny day when Miss Muffet decided to take her bowl of curds and whey to her favourite tuffet of grass under the oak tree.

Her ancestor Rip Van Winkle had planted the seed, then he lay down to sleep. When he awoke it was 100 years later and this lovely oak tree had sprouted from the little seed. She settled down with a sigh of happiness and looked around at her neighbours.

It was very peaceful, except for the children who lived with the old woman in the shoe. There were so many of them she just didn't know what to do with them.

Over the hill Jack and Jill climbed up the hill for a pail of water. They did look happy.

The crooked man was just coming out of his crooked house. She wondered why he always went on the crooked road, when he could have walked on the straight road.

Down on farmer Brown's yard there was a lot going on. The cat and the fiddle were trying to have a duet. It wasn't very tuneful. The cow was practising high jumps. He said he was going to jump over the moon. What nonsense. The little dog was lying on his back with laughter at these antics. While the dish and the spoon were running off down the road.

Suddenly she was aware of a movement at her side. She turned to look and there was a great big spider. She jumped in fright and lifted her foot to run, but stamped down hard on the annoying spider instead.

Nessie Shaw

CROAKED

It was a stupid thing to do. The moment she kissed the slimy frog she knew it was a mistake. What kind of prince did she expect from a lumpy, croaking, dirty brown amphibian? Vain, arrogant, patronising, but worst of all, cruel. After his recovery from his frog skin incarceration, he condescendingly allowed her to live at the palace, with a view to wedlock. He thought it a good match because she could not compete with him in the looks department. He spent many hours and a good deal of royal gold on lotions and potions to enhance, what he considered, his irresistible good looks. She managed a quick shower and hair up in a pony tail.

She could have borne his narcissism but it was his attitude to frogs she loathed. He hated them with a vengeance. He ordered all frogs exterminated. Frog hunting became the national sport. Trophies offered as prizes for the most frogs, the biggest frogs, different coloured frogs. They soon became an endangered species. Finally, they were so rare, that a prize of half the kingdom was offered for the next frog presented to the Grand Vizier.

She thought, then did what any sensible girl should. She e-mailed her granny. Granny replied *'Try www.granny'smagicspells/prince/frogs.'*

The rest was easy. She simply mentioned she had a new skin care cream she was trying out. The difficult part was persuading the Grand Vizier that she found the frog sitting in front of the prince's cheval mirror.

Sheila Wicks

FAMILY COMPLETE

You were a surprise, not planned at all
I already had one so very small
But, when you happened along,
A bond grew that became so strong
I thought my family was complete
A boy and a girl, nothing could compete
For all the times of joy and pleasure
Special times every mother should treasure
Visions of my daughter, caster oil in her hair
Tons of the stuff my son had put there!
As you both grew, another surprise
A second son, joy to my eyes
That was it now, no more for me
Because I was happy with just you three.

Trudi James

MY BOY

He breezed into my life one day
Couldn't believe my eyes -
At this bundle of sheer, pure joy
My baby boy surprise!
He grew up - loved his food
Was into this and that -
He taught me new technology
(And laughed at my old hats!)
He had his own computer
And would while away the hours
It was him who did the garden
And planted all my flowers.
As I grew older - he grew younger
He'd tease me many times -
And when the girlfriends came around
(I began to read all the signs!)
Of all the extra bathing -
The talc and aftershave,
'Do I look all right Mum?'
As he donned the latest craze!
The singing voice had ended
He was out the house so much,
He didn't want his 'old girl'
Who was completely out of touch -
With all his new life brought him
His clothes and bachelor den -
Taking second place to all the girls
And do I miss him?
Now and then!

Iris Cone

FALLING DOWN

Nappies, nipples and formula milk
Baby bottoms as smooth as silk
Infant kiss defies the noun
Tiny children have a way of falling down

F McFaul

HAIKUS OF LOVE

Mother's arm, soft-curved,
Her face: reflective, down-turned.
Baby yawns, then sleeps.

Curled hands are now still,
Wet eyelashes stop blinking.
No more weeping. Dream!

Mother, too, is tired.
Closes her eyes . . . yes: half smiles.
Joins her child in rest.

Quiet love palpitates -
Silently, they bond closely.
They are one, again.

Katharine Holmström